1983

Merry Christmas to
Julie + Joe . . . . . .
. . . . . to remind
you of the
daughter Success . . . . . .
Love,
Jennie's happy

B. TOBEY
OF
THE NEW YORKER

B. TOBEY
OF
THE NEW YORKER

DODD, MEAD & COMPANY

New York

THIS BOOK IS FOR
BEATRICE
DAVID
NANCY

Published by Dodd, Mead & Company, Inc.
79 Madison Avenue, New York, N.Y. 10016

Distributed in Canada by
McClelland and Stewart Limited, Toronto

Manufactured in the United States of America

FIRST EDITION

Library of Congress Cataloging in Publication Data

Tobey, B. (Barney)
B. Tobey of the New Yorker.

1. Caricatures and cartoons—United States—History—
20th century. 2. American wit and humor, Pictorial.
I. New Yorker (New York, N.Y.: 1925) II. Title.
NC1429.T55A4 1983   741.5'973   83-8948
ISBN 0-396-08195-9

INTRODUCTION

THE FIRST THING people are curious about is how do cartoonists get "ideas." I wish I knew. But I do know that it's important for a cartoonist to be irreverent and courageous.

There are many ways of working on ideas. I take a large drawing pad and before long the page is filled with doodles, thumbnail sketches, words, ink spots, and fantasies from my subconscious (see Appendix). It also helps to have nightmares, imagination, and a large dog to take out on exploring walks. Sometimes I get an idea reading a newspaper, or magazine, or listening to music. Travel is good, too. I remember an outdoor concert in Paris where the mosquitoes were particularly hungry. The conductor was leading his orchestra with a fly swatter! A cartoon was born.

I carry a small sketchbook in my pocket. Sometimes I walk to the Metropolitan Museum, which is nearby. One day I wandered into the large Persian room, filled with rare tapestries, vases, rugs, and other objets d'art. I overheard one woman say to another, "I just don't see how they can dust all this." It became a successful and interesting cartoon, and I enjoyed doing it.

I bring my rough cartoon ideas to Lee Lorenz, the art editor of *The New Yorker*. He may comment, suggest a change in a drawing or a caption, and then show them to William Shawn, the editor of the magazine.

Many years ago, when Harold Ross was editor, he was asked why he didn't use color in the cartoons. His answer, now famous, was, "What's so funny about red?" I agree. In fact, I see the world in black and white.

I still find New York City a magnificent and exciting city to walk around and sketch in.

In school I was lucky in my art teachers. One of them made us pose for each other, instead of the basket of wax fruit. I was awarded a scholarship to Parson's Art School, but left after a year to work at Batten, Barton, Durstine & Osborn's advertising agency. I stayed six years. It was great training for me. I did layouts, lettering, photo retouching, and advertisements. Eventually, I was made head of the art department. After hours at the agency I tried three covers for *The New Yorker*. They were bought. That settled it! I decided to freelance, to do commercial art, and most of all, cartoons for *The New Yorker*. I attended the Art Students League at night. Boardman Robinson, one of my instructors, made us walk around the block and come back to draw what we remembered. It's something I've never forgotten.

My father was always encouraging and later proudly papered the entire wall space of his paper and twine store with tear sheets of my cartoons.

There's no best way of working. I've worked in the art department of an agency, in a large studio with other cartoonists, and alone in a studio. Finally, I worked at home, which I still do. But it is lonely.

It's not difficult to draw a cartoon, but is difficult to have a fresh idea, as well as a drawing with humor, and quality, and general interest.

The New Yorker always refers to their cartoonists as "our artists," and original cartoon drawings are being bought by collectors. Cartoons have a venerable tradition, like the works of Hogarth, Rowlandson, Daumier, and Cruikshank. Their drawings expressed the life of their times. *The New Yorker* artists are expressing with wit and humor a visual chronicle of the changing life style of our times!

BARNEY TOBEY
New York City, 1983

"Well, Emmeline, what's new?"

"*Do you know what this means to me? It means from now on, when I have something to say, people are going to listen.*"

"Don't you know *anything* but 'Afternoon of a Faun'?"

"Gerald has always felt strongly about encouraging young artists."

"His Royal Highness was a night person."

"*Why, no, I didn't see any fox go past here.*"

"Sanford, the city is proceeding without us."

"*Remember, now—you've got to show him who's boss.*"

"It means that Santa's coming to town."

B TOBEY

"*Man does not live by pemmican alone, Baby.*"

"May we?"

B TOBEY

"The Graysons are on vacation in Europe. I'm the sitter."

"*Pardon us, gentlemen, but how would you like to be in a film about life in America today?*"

"Then what happened?"

"I want her first marriage to be a beautiful one."

"Congratulations, keep moving, please. Congratulations, keep moving, please. Congratulations . . ."

"But, Paul, is anybody ever really happy?"

"Edgar? Have you been waiting long?"

"We only have ninety minutes, so we needn't try to copy it exactly."

B.TOBEY.

"George, would you mind if we sat somewhere else?"

"We mustn't forget the saltwater taffy for Aunt Edith."

"Are you all right, Mister? Is there anything I can do?"

"Young man, you're the only one who bothered to stop! I'm a millionaire and I'm going to give you five thousand dollars!"

"Now, there's a warm human being for you!"

"We've already done this room. I remember that fire extinguisher."

"Eight hundred and fifty years old! I guess we *have* to check it out."

"*You know, Henry, I'd never think of feeding the pigeons in Central Park!*"

"I've got thousands and thousands of constituents, but no friends."

"*Strange. Twenty-four years later, and I still think of this as the cocktail hour.*"

"We don't have a song yet."

"*This is the time of year I wish I wasn't a bum.*"

"I guess if they'd had baseball in
olden times the Mets would have played here."

"We can't pay taxes, but give our best regards to the King and Queen."

"Mother!"

"Larry, is there anything I can do?"

"In my time, I was considered a Don Juan. How about you?"

"One important fact we must never lose sight of, gentlemen—we are
making it at a time when they're letting us keep it."

"Never heard of him."

"*Good afternoon, ladies and gentlemen. The course is 'The Roots of the English Novel.' I'm Professor Fowles, and I assume all of you can read and write.*"

"It's over, Manuel. Can't you see? It's _over_."

"*What a relief not to have to fiddle around adjusting the flesh tones.*"

"*Ed, remember my barn when it had cows in it?*"

"*Have a good day!*"

"*Of course you don't understand it. He's an artists' artist.*"

"I want you to promise me something. No matter how fantastic my offer, promise you won't sell that thing to me later in the evening."

"Is there a ruin with a roof?"

"*I suppose I don't <u>dare</u> order iced tea.*"

"All right, but promise you'll come in and go to bed the instant you <u>do</u> discover the meaning of it all."

"Starting at the left, Marini, David Smith, Giacometti, Stankiewicz, Calder, Nevelson, and, good Lord, my wife and Harvey Peterson!"

"*You're in top form tonight, Luigi.*"

"*Me? Oh, no. I'm just looking for a man.*"

"He's busy now, Doctor. Can you come back later?"

"*Miss Craig, I've cleaned up my desk. I am now going to lunch.*"

"*Cream cheese and jelly on white, to take out.*"

"Please don't use that joke about our vegetable garden being at the A. & P."

"*We were here ten years ago. That was the time we went to Harry's Bar and Roger fell in the Grand Canal.*"

"*Stand erect, feet twelve inches apart. Now bend forward to touch floor between feet—try to keep knees straight.*"

"The ambiance is great! The blazing fire is great! The service is great! The food is great! The wine is great! You're great! I'm great!"

"*Would you mind taking off your glasses, Marlene? I want to have a serious talk with you.*"

"*Oh, Sally, you know—What's-His-Name. The artist who does this sort of thing.*"

"When you need a cop, there's never one around."

"*Very good, Mrs. Simmons. I think you're ready for a larger canvas.*"

"If he says 'Upsy-daisy' once more, I'm going to dump him in the ditch!"

"This neighborhood sure has changed since I was a kid."

"*I know more about art
than you do, so I'll tell you what to like.*"

"*Madam, you're mistaken! I definitely was <u>not</u> tickling your neck!*"

"*Please*, Donald, promise you won't try to use your credit card tonight."

"All I see is more trees."

"*I don't know anything about art, but this is a damned good Martini.*"

"*The feature goes on at six-ten, eight-ten, and ten-ten.*"

"*Guess who made the pâté.*"

"*Fantastic, J.T.! What a backdrop for a sitcom.*"

"Dynamite, Maura! It's now, it's you, and it's credible!"

"*I may not know much about corporate-tax law,*
but I damn well know what I like."

"Oh, so that's why your grass is greener than mine. It's plastic."

"*Well, there she goes—right on the dot.*"

"*Madam, you have a very, very, very wrong number.*"

"On second thought, I do have a
message for mankind: Nuts to one and nuts to all!"

"Looks like a great year for this vineyard!"

"Oh, for goodness' sake, Dick! Come off it!"

"Tell me, Agnes, just what the hell <u>have</u> you been knitting all these years?"

"If it's not the goddam summer people, it's the goddam winter people!"

"*I wish I could describe it to you, Herb—the sun pouring a flood of gold into the valley, the lake set like a sapphire amid the denser green of the trees, the hills of more tragic cast, rolling off to the horizon in rich, purple undulations.*"

"*He looks pleased with himself. If I find out why, I'll call you later.*"

"*Before we start, I think you should know we're surrounded by poison ivy.*"

"Yoo-hoo! How's the water?"

"*Do you know what would be nice, Matthew? It would be nice if we had a few firecrackers.*"

"*I want to learn Italian and she wants to learn English.*"

"Not a thing about tomorrow's weather."

"Not on your life! Come and get it."

"Why can't *you* ever think of a socko exit line?"

"... except ours had a shorter tail and slightly longer ears."

"Oh, Claude! Not <u>another</u> one!"

"*No, I've never been to Paris. In fact, I've
never been out of the States.*"

"What I mean is _aside_ from all the others, is there anyone else?"

"*Looking at us objectively, I'd say we were really quite stunning creatures.*"

"*One* of us is fast."

"Where's _my_ chair?"

"What will it be? A taco, an eggroll, a falafel—or just a plain hot dog?"

"Well, tell me. Is this Aztec, Mayan, Olmec, or Toltec?"

"*What a wife! Night after night,
she sits there and reads the sports page to him.*"

"Last I heard, he was living in a trailer camp off Route 212."

"No, you certainly may _not_ have a hamburger!"

"*Don't you think it's time you put your jacket on?*"

"*I would like a tube of lemon yellow, cadmium red, cobalt blue, ivory, black, and zinc white, a sixteen-by-twenty canvas, a couple of brushes, and that book 'Painting in Oils.'*"

"Oh, for God's sake, Jerry! Pick a card."

"*I hope you don't mind. We just couldn't get a sitter.*"

"*He used to paint there on weekends. Now he only uses it to sulk.*"

"*You should have come along. Everybody we know is down there.*"

"Another nice thing about Venice—no potholes!"

"Damn it, Wilbur, that's _our_ bench!"

"*I can't understand you, Harold. Why is it you're the only
one who doesn't know it's spring?*"

"Sit up straight!"

"*As usual!*"

"*Gosh, thanks, honey! If I discover a new star, I'll name it after you.*"

APPENDIX

THE MAKING OF A CARTOON—I

*"Let's roll up our sleeves and get to it, gentlemen—we have
to spend billions and billions and billions!"*

The situation of the military *idea* came with doodles on large sheets of paper.

I was lucky with the Pentagon cartoon. I've always sketched characters in buses, subways, parks, etc. Then one day, reading the newspaper and worrying about disarmament, I thought of a large table, and seated around it were some of my sketchbook people, some smug, some pleased with themselves, some miserable—only they were transformed into Pentagon Chiefs of Staff. Most were in uniform, exaggerated with bright ribbons and gold medals. The Chief of Staff looked deliriously happy and said, "Gentlemen, we have to spend billions and billions . . ." It became a shorthand editorial cartoon.

The Pentagon
U.S. Defense
The Vice President

Joint Chiefs of Staff
Joint Chief of Staff
the generals —
Generals

Poet
Poetry

To buy a spring suit = shoes
Summer

Men with beards —
" without "

In Supermarket

BEER

yng coupl

MARCH APRIL MAY

march 17
Parade
St. Patrick's
DAY

JUNE

all this
Crab Grass

with a college diploma like that — your
son deserves — a great frame

It's one of those rare
spring days when I'm
glad I don't have a job —
I have to go to work

FRAMING

→ he deserves a
good frame

He has a college diploma

once in a lifetime — you
should be proud — and

Wood carving

some of
them are
ZEROX

wall doctor's
office — lots of
diplomas

Remember, your son's
college diploma happens
once in a lifetime —

"*Let's roll up our sleeves and get to it, gentlemen—we have to spend billions and billions and billions!*"

"What I really feel like having is ham and eggs."

I was walking on a street filled with a variety of ethnic restaurants. I watched the people studying the menus in the windows, wondering which was the best place to eat.

When I got back to my studio I made notes on colorful ethnic restaurants, people strolling about. How to use them? Then I thought of a young couple, tired of fancy gourmet ethnic food and wanting something simple. How would they look? Angry? Happy? Hungry? I tried a small, loose sketch of the couple walking and the young man saying to the girl, "I want something simple like ham and eggs."

I saw it clearly enough, and with my notes was able to do the drawing from memory.

725-4790
RUTH B.
PREMIUM DUE
INSURANCE

lon J Mae?
Was child
Prodigy —
and then
what?

The Food is Terrible
but they have
six tennis courts

· In hammock
SUMMER —
Tanglewood
the Shed

a pool-side chat

Mozart

Vacation Cottage
in the woods?
on a lake —
outboard motor

Where to eat?

IDEA — have to develope — should be interesting + funny.
The problem: where to eat?

The usual — they want hamburgers.

"The most of us don't like Sushi!"

"Let's take a vote. Who's for eating Chinese?"

The situation: A whole long street of restaurants — —

"What I really feel like having is ham and eggs."

"*What I __really__ feel like having is ham and eggs.*"